HOW IT HAPPENS
at the TV Station

By Shawndra Shofner
Photographs by Bob and Diane Wolfe

CLARA HOUSE BOOKS

Minneapolis

The publisher would like to thank the employees of WCCO TV for their generous help with this book. All photogaphs by Bob and Diane Wolfe except page 28 (bottom), WCCO.

Clara House Books
The Oliver Press, Inc.
Charlotte Square
5707 West 36th Street
Minneapolis, MN 55416-2510

Publisher Cataloging Information

Shofner, Shawndra
        How it happens at the TV station / by Shawndra Shofner ; photographs by Bob and Diane Wolfe.
                p.   cm.
        Includes index.
        ISBN 978-1-934545-07-2
        Summary: Text and photographs tell of the different people who are a part of a television newscast and some of the special equipment used to produce television news.
        1. Television broadcasting of news—Juvenile literature   2. Television broadcasting of news—Vocational guidance—Juvenile literature   3. Television stations—Employees—Juvenile literature   [1. Television broadcasting of news   2. Occupations]   I. Wolfe, Robert L.   II. Wolfe, Diane   III. Title   IV. Title: At the TV station
        070.1/95—dc22

ISBN 978-1-934545-07-2
Printed in the United States of America
12 11 10 09   4 3 2 1

Every day, millions of people turn on the TV news. Some want information about politics. Others tune in for weather reports. Still others watch the newscasts to learn about special events and local projects. Just what does it take to put on a newscast? Let's go behind the scenes at one station to find out. Lights! Camera! Action!

News Production

The assignment desk is where the action begins in this newsroom. News assignment editors are people who collect story ideas 24 hours a day, seven days a week. Story ideas come in by telephone, email, and police and fire scanners. It's important for assignment editors to know what's happening in their community. They do this by surfing the Internet, reading newspapers, and watching other televised news programs.

The assignment board keeps the entire newsroom informed about what stories are being covered, by whom, and where. If breaking news comes in, for example, about a building fire or car crash, the board helps the assignment editors find the closest **reporter** to send to cover the story.

TIME	STORY	CREW
	ROSEMOUNT FATAL	MOLENDA / SOIE
	HOME LOANS	CHANEY / SONYA
	GUITAR HERO	BISS / LAURITSEN
	ROSEMOUNT FATA.	GOIE / DARCY
	ST. PATRICKS DAY	KOPP / MAYA
	DOG: OUTDOORS	NEUSWANTER/KESSLER
	HFR: OAK ST	MEARS/REGER
	DOME SHECHECK/RSS	MEARS
	AM SHOOT	CONAN / ANGELA
		CONAN
		MOLENDA

The station's staff of assignment editors, reporters, **producers,** and **anchors** gathers every day at 10:00 AM and 2:30 PM to talk about what stories they should cover for upcoming newscasts. They each bring in as many story ideas as they can think of. All of the ideas are written on a white board. They discuss each idea and decide which ones are better than others. By the end of the meeting, they will have agreed on what stories—or **assignments**—the reporters will cover.

Reporters work at their desks in a large open space called the newsroom. There they make telephone calls, do computer research, and write stories.

Reporters are the station's staff members who gather information for stories. They often travel with news photographers to places where news is happening. They give up-to-the-minute details of news events in front of a camera. In these live shots, reporters describe what is happening, often questioning people at the scene. Reporters also set up and do interviews, which are filmed by a news photographer.

Editors take the video tapes of reporters' interviews and edit them, choosing which parts will make up the story. Usually, only a small part of a reporter's interviews makes it into the story that is seen on TV.

Technical Production

The control room is where many people work together to combine the pieces of the newscast to complete the show. The newscast's producer decides what content, or stories, will make up the newscast. The director of the newscast makes sure that everything that goes into it—live shots, graphics, and stories that were recorded earlier—follow the producer's plan.

Technical directors are the people who put on the screen the images that you see at home. To do this, they operate a machine called a switcher. The switcher has more than 1,000 knobs and switches.

Audio engineers mix sound to the video that will be shown during the newscast. They can make sounds louder or softer and add different effects, such as music.

Tapes for commercials, TV shows, and recorded newscasts are stored on a server in the tape room. During a newscast, the tape room engineer also plays the stories that the reporter recorded earlier in the day.

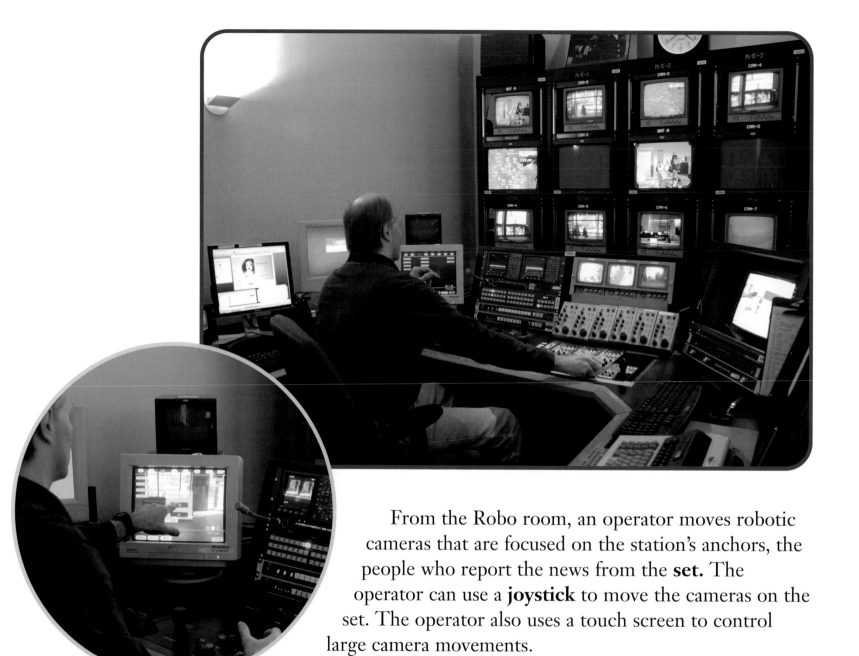

From the Robo room, an operator moves robotic cameras that are focused on the station's anchors, the people who report the news from the **set.** The operator can use a **joystick** to move the cameras on the set. The operator also uses a touch screen to control large camera movements.

Air control operators make sure everything the station plans to show on TV actually gets on the air. They follow instructions that tell them when programs, commercials, newscasts, and anything else are scheduled to appear on the air. If there is a problem with the station's signal, an engineer looks for the cause of the problem and fixes it.

On the Air

Anchors report the news, meteorologists prepare
weather reports and forecasts, and sportscasters
interview athletes and give scores. These people you
see on your TV are called the talent.

TV anchors talk to cameras as if they were talking to another person. Tally lights on the cameras light up to show the anchors which camera they should look into.

Anchors report the news while seated on the set. They usually sit on swivel chairs behind a large desk, facing the cameras.

The IFB (interruptible feedback) system uses a device similar to the earbuds that people listen to music with on their MP3 players. Anchors wear an IFB earpiece so that they can hear directions from the producer and director. They also clip microphones to their shirt. The microphones send their voices to the audio engineer.

Anchors rarely look down at the paper scripts in front of them. Rather, they use a machine called a teleprompter. Teleprompters reflect large-print copies of the news script onto a one-way mirror. Anchors read the sentences as they scroll down the mirror. A camera behind the mirror films the speakers, who appear to be looking right at newscast viewers.

The teleprompter operator controls the speed at which the words appear. Some people speak faster than others, so it's the teleprompter operator's job to make sure that the words appearing on the teleprompter do not go faster or slower than the anchor speaks.

This is the flash-cam set. Anchors sometimes use this set for live interviews or special feature stories.

Many lights hang from the ceiling of the sets. These lights brighten the set to allow its shadows and colors to pop. Light readings are taken to make sure that the lighting is adjusted to highlight the anchors and the set.

Anchors like to look their best before they go on the air to start their newscasts. They get ready in the green room, where they apply make-up and fix their hair.

The Weather Center

The weather center is a very important part of the TV station. Meteorologists report the day's weather and prepare forecasts for the days ahead. The meteorologist uses computers to create maps and images that will help to report the weather.

Meteorologists study weather patterns and maps to determine what their forecasts will be. They know that many viewers rely on weather forecasts to work in their gardens, make travel plans or, if a snowstorm is coming, prepare to stay home.

Meteorologists broadcast live in front of a large green screen. Viewers at home do not see the green screen because engineers in the control room use computer technology to remove all green color from the screen. They replace the color with maps and images.

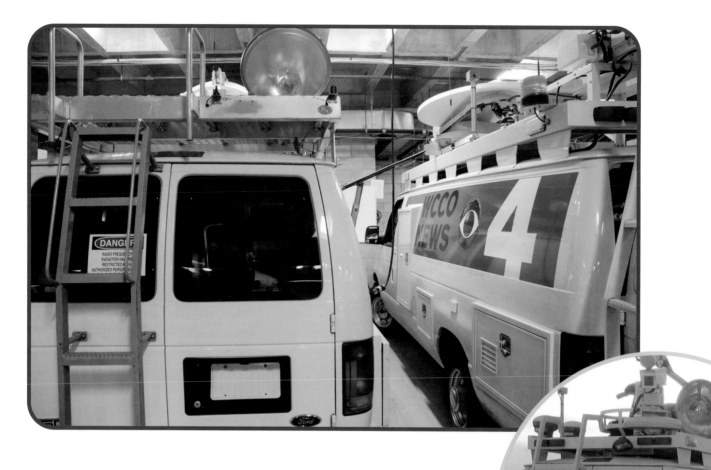

Special Contributors

The station's satellite trucks travel great distances if that is what is needed to cover a story. From the trucks, reporters' stories are beamed to satellites high in the sky and then transmitted, or sent down, to the station.

Satellite trucks are loaded with the audio and video equipment that reporters need to transmit their stories, which often are broadcast live during newscasts.

Graphic designers create the illustrations that you see on TV. Using computers, they draw charts or pictures that add something extra to reporters' stories.

Wrap

It takes many people working together in the building to deliver the newscasts that you watch on TV at home. From beginning to end, their goal is to make your viewing experience informative and enjoyable.

Glossary

Anchors – the station's people who lead broadcasts and appear on TV

Assignments – story ideas for news reports that reporters are given

Joystick – a lever that allows operators to move TV cameras on the set

Producers – the people who are in charge of a news broadcast from beginning to end

Reporters – staff members at the station who gather information for stories

Set – the area at the station from which anchors and meteorologists broadcast

Index

Websites

www.wcco.com
http://www.weeklyreader.com/kidsnews/

WITHDRAWN